Passages OF Light

Selected Scriptures with Reflections by

THOMAS KINKADE

Painter of Light™

★ *The Great American Century* ★

THOMAS NELSON PUBLISHERS
Nashville

Passages
OF *Light*

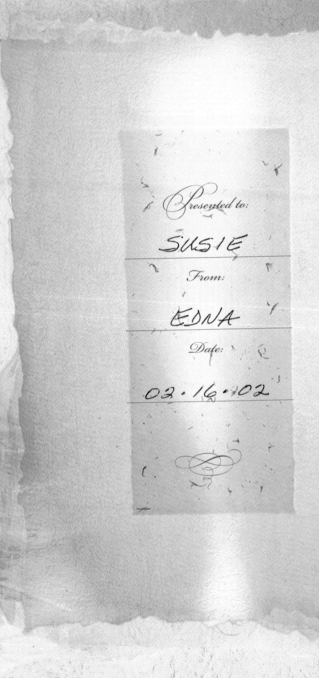

Presented to:

SUSIE

From:

EDNA

Date:

02 · 16 · 02

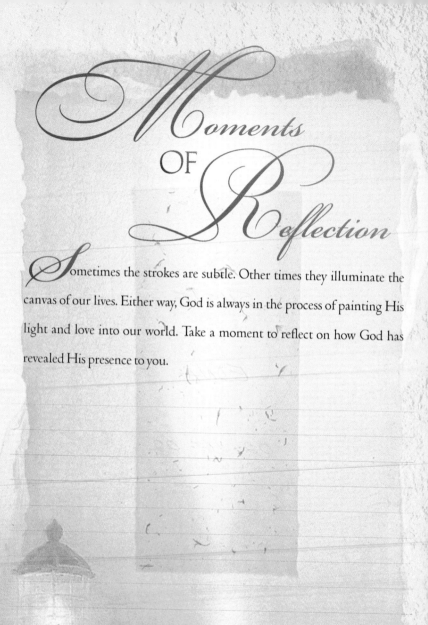

Moments OF Reflection

Sometimes the strokes are subtle. Other times they illuminate the canvas of our lives. Either way, God is always in the process of painting His light and love into our world. Take a moment to reflect on how God has revealed His presence to you.

Contents

Thomas
Kinkade

Gallery OF Paintings

Light OF THE Word

Light OF Life

Light OF *Hope*

Light OF *Creation*

Light OF THE _World_

Light OF _Grace_

A Message OF Light, Hope & Love

BY THOMAS KINKADE

There is nothing more glorious than the morning—when the first rays of light break through the trees and set the world on course for the day's activities. It is the time when I meet with God and see the radiance of His glory—that first introduction of light into life that fires my spirit and kindles the joy that burns throughout the day. It is the essence of hope you see in my paintings, and that inspires my attraction to light in my work.

But there was a time when the picture of my life was not so bright. Just as night precedes the break of dawn, so I found my soul in a spiritual darkness that cast its shadow on my work. Growing up, I had always had a fascination with light—the way it reflected off the wet pavement and shone in the streets from lampposts and houses. But my renderings lacked luster. Like the work of so many artists, themes of sadness and pain seemed more prolific than hope, and it came out in the paintings. My vision was narrow, focused on my private motives, delivering a more superficial message that, while artful, still betrayed my deepest longings.

*T*hen morning came when the radiant light of Christ penetrated the darkness of my heart with His love. His joy. His hope. And it poured out of my life onto the canvas with a vibrancy I had never seen before. I call it "The Anointing," for in a real way, as I was saved, so was my art. I began to see that art is not about me. It's about communicating with someone else—about blessing, uplifting, and touching other people's lives with God's message of hope. A hope that is not limited to canvas, but that is true in our lives when we walk in the light of His Word.

$\mathcal{I}$ am excited about *Passages of Light* because the very words of God which inspire my work are available right beside the paintings. It's like getting two pictures in one—the picture of God's love and plan for us as He reveals Himself through Scripture, and also how He visually discloses His heart to us through the radiance of light in the world. While I didn't know this back when I was first drawn to paint light, God later showed me that the attraction was no accident. Light is an expression of His character—of who He is. If you study Scripture for any length of time, you can't help but see God define Himself in terms of light. Christ Himself said that He is the Light of the World. And in turn, He has called us as His children to be "lights in the world."

It is my hope that as you turn the pages of *Passages of Light*, you will discover the same joy in your own life that is found in my paintings—not an unattainable idealism, but the real hope, joy, light, and love that is pictured in God's Word and provided to us through His Son.

$\mathcal{S}$o come close, and bask in the warmth of God's love. Invite your family to feel the Bible in their hands and experience the awesome privilege of holding, in written form, the very expression of God Himself. And let the beauty of His work fire the hope in your own heart and home that lights the way for others to follow.

Thomas Kinkade

Light
OF THE
Word

I paint the world with lights, because that is how we see it. Without light, we would never know the colors of the rainbow, or see our reflection in the faces of our children. We would not know where we came from, and we would not know where we're going.

The same is true in the spiritual realm. Like luminaries lighting the pathway home, God's Word lights the way to life as He intended it to be — full of beauty and joy, peace and hope.

By living according to the light of His Word, our days are brighter, and the pathway home is clear.

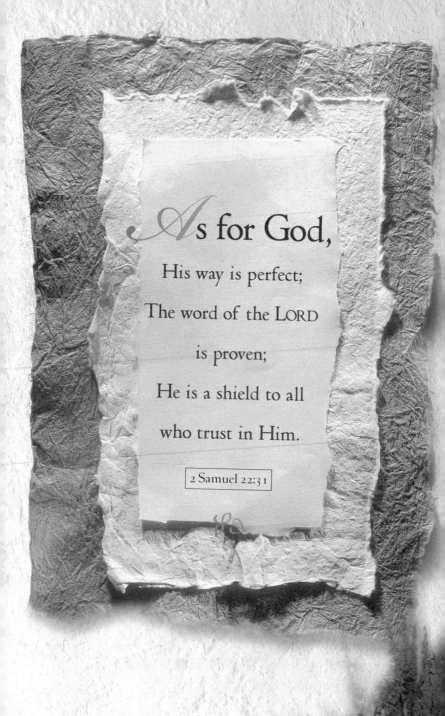

As for God,

His way is perfect;

The word of the LORD

is proven;

He is a shield to all

who trust in Him.

2 Samuel 22:31

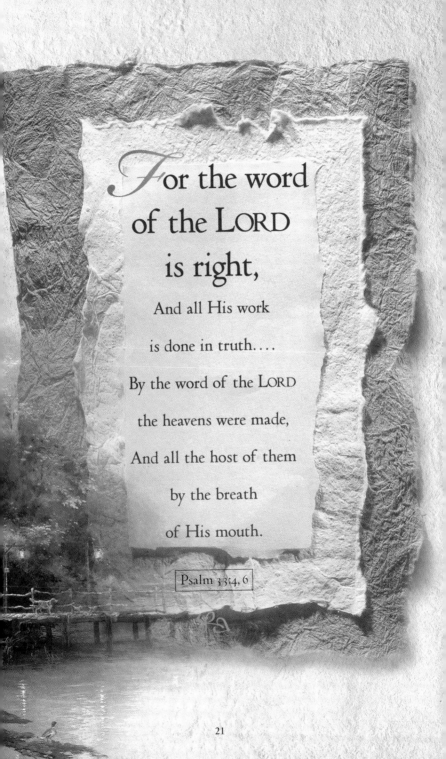

For the word
of the LORD
is right,

And all His work

is done in truth....

By the word of the LORD

the heavens were made,

And all the host of them

by the breath

of His mouth.

Psalm 33:4, 6

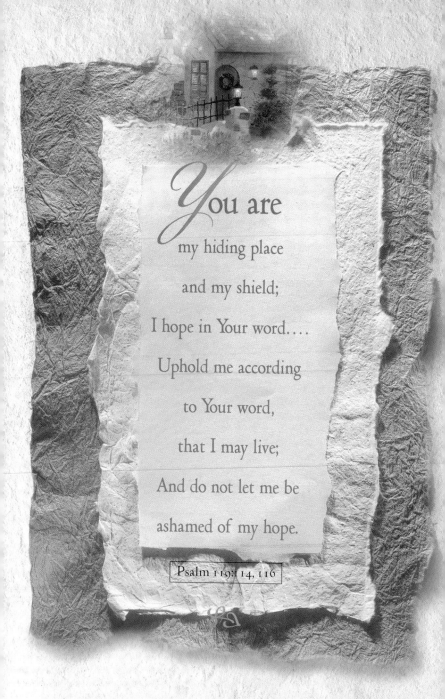

*Y*ou are

my hiding place

and my shield;

I hope in Your word....

Uphold me according

to Your word,

that I may live;

And do not let me be

ashamed of my hope.

Psalm 119:114, 116

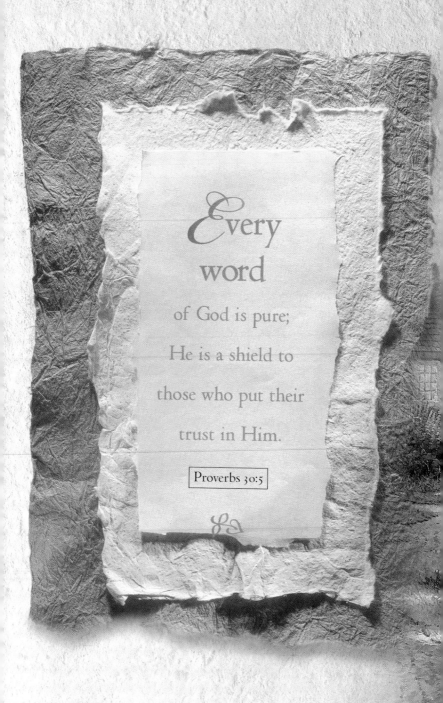

Every word of God is pure; He is a shield to those who put their trust in Him.

Proverbs 30:5

Thomas Kinkade

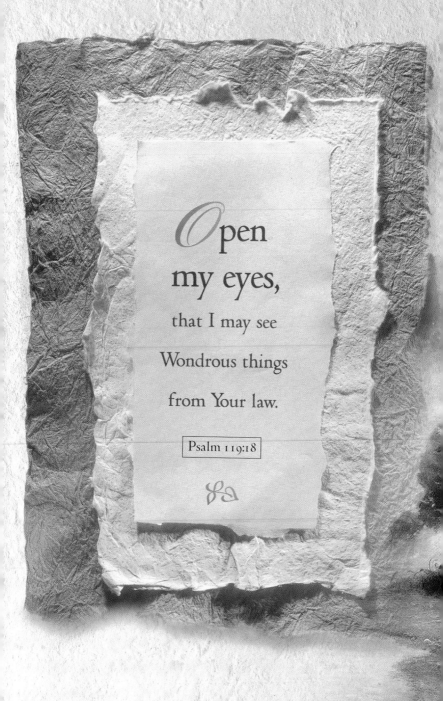

Open
my eyes,
that I may see
Wondrous things
from Your law.

Psalm 119:18

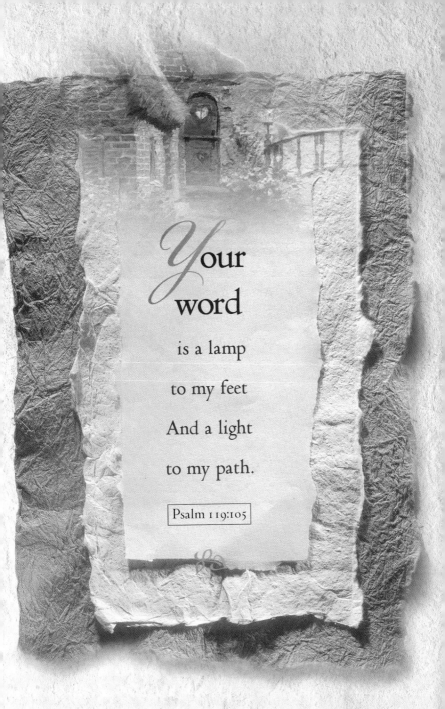

Your
word

is a lamp

to my feet

And a light

to my path.

Psalm 119:105

The
entrance
of Your words
gives light;
It gives understanding
to the simple.

Psalm 119:130

Thomas
Kinkade

Light
OF
Life

It isn't just the mansions that make it onto my canvas. More often, it's the humble cottage, the seasoned home, made special by the light and lives within.

I imagine God's canvas to be full of much the same—His masterpiece a portrait of children in sundry shapes, sizes, abilities, and hopes—all who gently, quietly, radiate the glory of the One who made them.

It is not the vessel that impresses, but the alluring light of Christ that draws inside those who stand in the dark.

For you were

once darkness,

but now you are light

in the Lord.

Walk as children

of light.

Ephesians 5:8

*T*hen Jesus spoke to them again, saying, "I am the light of the world. He who follows Me shall not walk in darkness, but have the light of life."

John 8:12

He has shown you,

O man, what is good;

And what does the LORD

require of you

But to do justly,

To love mercy,

And to walk humbly

with your God?

Micah 6:8

Oh, send out Your light

and Your truth!

Let them lead me;

Let them bring me to

Your holy hill

And to Your tabernacle.

Psalm 43:3

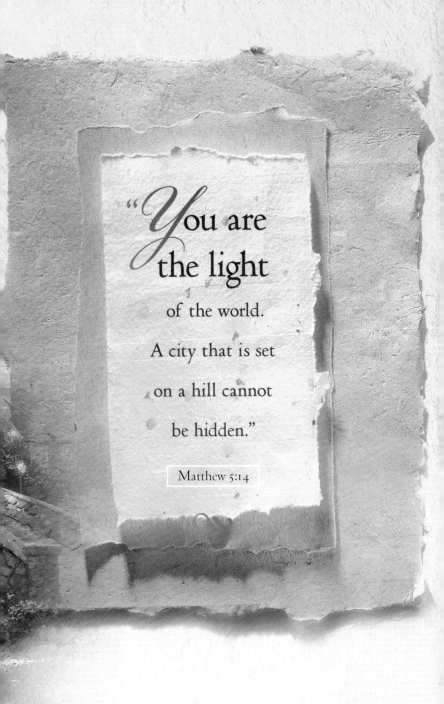

"*You are the light* of the world.

A city that is set

on a hill cannot

be hidden."

Matthew 5:14

The LORD is my shepherd;

I shall not want.

He makes me to lie down

in green pastures;

He leads me beside

the still waters.

He restores my soul;

He leads me in

the paths of righteousness

For His name's sake.

Psalm 23:1-3

Thomas Kinkade

Commit
your way
to the LORD,

Trust also in Him,

And He shall bring it to pass.

He shall bring forth

your righteousness

as the light,

And your justice

as the noonday.

Psalm 37:5, 6

Through the trees, the peaceful streams, the gentle rays of light, my hope unfolds on canvas—a hope for a better world for my children and of a future hope in heaven.

I know such yearnings are not in vain. God paints the same optimistic picture in His Word and makes my hope sure through His Son.

Though at times the picture of life seems misshapen—with lines disjointed and colors clashing—God sees a different beauty. It's simply my job to trust His design and await with anticipation the unveiling of His final masterpiece.

Thomas Kinkade

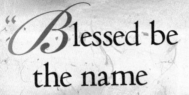

"Blessed be
the name

of God forever and ever,

For wisdom and might are His.

And He changes the times and the seasons;

He removes kings and raises up kings;

He gives wisdom to the wise

And knowledge to those

who have understanding.

He reveals deep and secret things;

He knows what is in the darkness,

And light dwells with Him."

Daniel 2:20b-22

Therefore my heart

is glad, and my glory rejoices;

My flesh also will rest in hope....

You will show me the path of life;

In Your presence is fullness of joy;

At Your right hand

are pleasures forevermore.

Psalm 16:9, 11

And there shall be

no more curse,

but the throne of God

and of the Lamb shall be in it,

and His servants shall serve Him....

There shall be no night there:

They need no lamp

nor light of the sun,

for the Lord God gives them light.

And they shall reign

forever and ever.

Revelation 22:3, 5

For I know

the thoughts that I think

toward you, says the LORD,

thoughts of peace

and not of evil,

to give you a future and a hope.

Then you will call upon Me

and go and pray to Me,

and I will listen to you.

And you will seek Me and find Me,

when you search for Me

with all your heart.

Jeremiah 29:11-13

"Blessed is the man who trusts in the LORD,

And whose hope is the LORD.

For he shall be like a tree

planted by the waters,

Which spreads out its roots by the river,

And will not fear when heat comes;

But its leaf will be green,

And will not be anxious

in the year of drought,

Nor will cease from yielding fruit."

Jeremiah 17:7, 8

$\mathcal{B}$e of
good courage,

And He shall

strengthen your heart,

All you who hope

in the LORD.

Psalm 31:24

Therefore,

having been justified by faith,

we have peace with God

through our Lord Jesus Christ,

through whom also

we have access by faith

into this grace

in which we stand,

and rejoice in hope

of the glory of God.

Romans 5:1, 2

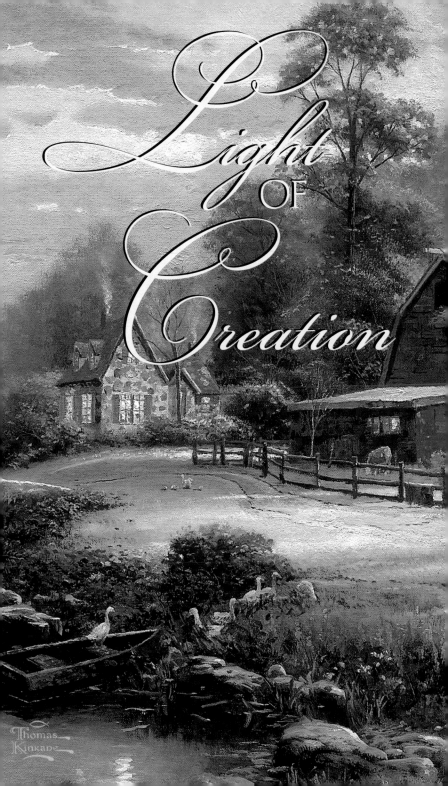

Light

OF

Creation

For me, it's easy to see God smile. I need only to look at the nearest tree, the closest bloom, the simplest cloud to see His pleasure. And that's why nature plays such a lively role in my paintings.

As my various works reveal different clues to the deepest parts of my soul, so God gives us a glimpse of His heart through all that He's made—from the majesty of the mountains to the still, quiet voice of the stream.

By painting His creation, I begin to capture the color of God.

For behold,

He who forms mountains,

And creates the wind,

Who declares to man

what his thought is,

And makes the morning darkness,

Who treads the high places

of the earth–

The LORD God of hosts

is His name.

Amos 4:13

The heavens
declare
the glory of God;
And the firmament
shows His handiwork.

Psalm 19:1

Light

OF

Hope

$\mathcal{I}$ will open rivers

in desolate heights,

And fountains in the midst of the valleys;

I will make the wilderness

a pool of water,

And the dry land springs of water....

That they may see and know,

And consider and understand together,

That the hand of the LORD

has done this,

And the Holy One of Israel

has created it.

Isaiah 41:18, 20

Thomas Kinkade

"*Fear not,*

for I have redeemed you;

I have called you by your name;

You are Mine.

When you pass through the waters,

I will be with you;

And through the rivers,

they shall not overflow you....

For I am the LORD your God,

The Holy One of Israel, your Savior;...

Since you were precious in My sight,

You have been honored,

And I have loved you."

Isaiah 43:1b-4

For since the creation

of the world

His invisible attributes

are clearly seen,

being understood

by the things that are made,

even His eternal power

and Godhead,

so that they are without excuse.

Romans 1:20

Bless the LORD,

O my soul! O LORD my God,

You are very great:

You are clothed

with honor and majesty,

Who cover Yourself with light

as with a garment,

Who stretch out the heavens

like a curtain.

He lays the beams of His upper chambers

in the waters,

Who makes the clouds His chariot,

Who walks on the wings of the wind,

Who makes His angels spirits,

His ministers a flame of fire.

Psalm 104:1-4

"Listen to this, O Job;

Stand still and consider

the wondrous works of God.

Do you know when God dispatches them,

And causes the light of His cloud to shine?

Do you know how the clouds are balanced,

Those wondrous works of Him

who is perfect in knowledge?…

He comes from the north

as golden splendor;

With God is awesome majesty."

Job 37:14-16, 22

*H*e didn't come in a blaze of glory. (That will happen the second time.) Over the sleeping town of Bethlehem, God chose a single star to herald the moment and light the way to the long-awaited Messiah. Born in a manger, the Light of the World had come.

And the world would never be the same.

Today, when I look up at the stars, I see more than a warm glow in the night. I also see God's plan of hope—His Son—shining still.

If I take the wings of the morning,

And dwell in the uttermost parts of the sea,

Even there Your hand shall lead me,

And Your right hand shall hold me.

If I say, "Surely the darkness shall fall on me,"

Even the night shall be light about me;

Indeed, the darkness

shall not hide from You,

But the night shines as the day;

The darkness and the light

are both alike to You.

Psalm 139:9-12

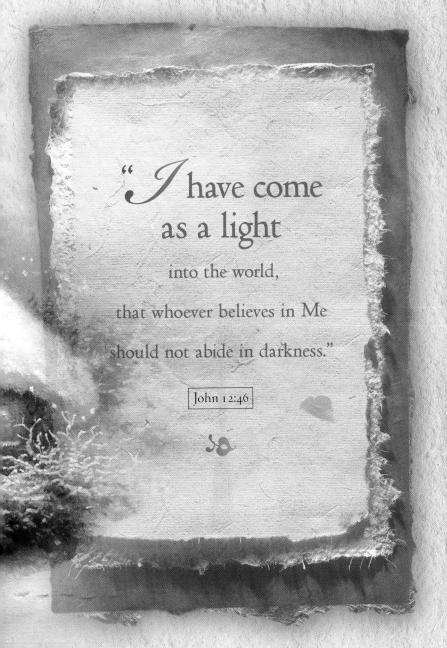

"I have come
as a light

into the world,

that whoever believes in Me

should not abide in darkness."

John 12:46

Every
good gift

and every perfect gift

is from above,

and comes down

from the Father of lights,

with whom there is

no variation

or shadow of turning.

James 1:17

Thomas Kinkade

And the Word

became flesh

and dwelt among us,

and we beheld His glory,

the glory as of the only

begotten of the Father,

full of grace and truth.

John 1:14

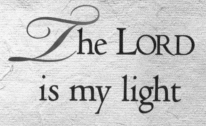

The LORD
is my light

and my salvation;

Whom shall I fear?

The LORD is the strength

of my life;

Of whom shall I be afraid?

Psalm 27:1

Thomas
Kinkade

Your mercy, O LORD,

is in the heavens;

Your faithfulness

reaches to the clouds.

Your righteousness

is like the great mountains;

Your judgments are a great deep;

O LORD,

You preserve man and beast.

Psalm 36:5, 6

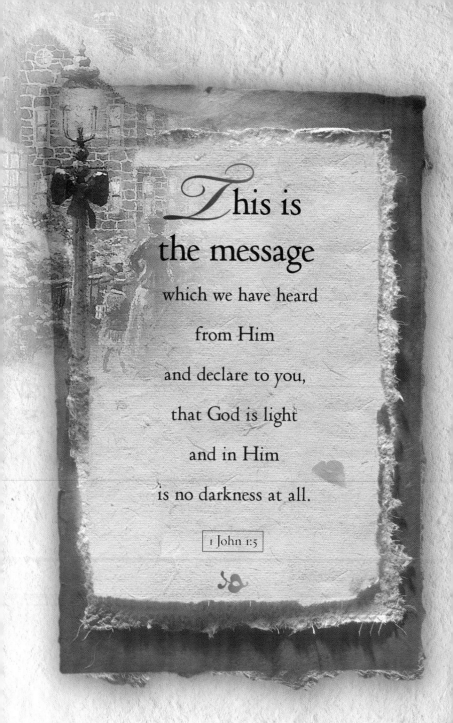

$\mathscr{T}$his is
the message
which we have heard

from Him

and declare to you,

that God is light

and in Him

is no darkness at all.

1 John 1:5

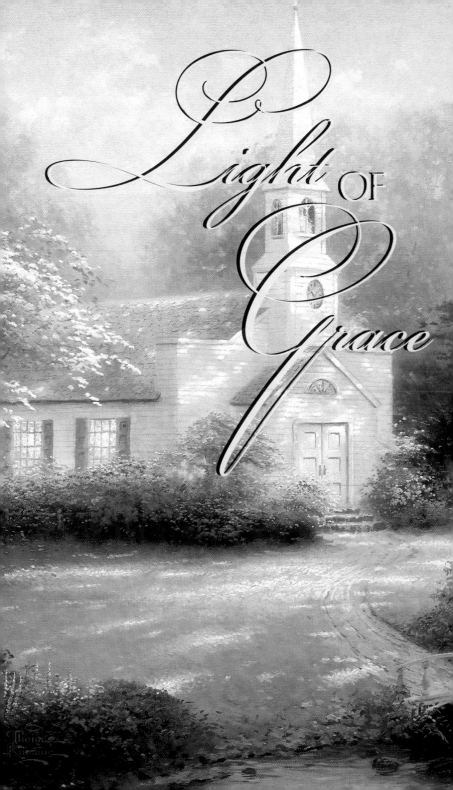

I love the light of springtime. The way dew dances in the early morning sun. The brilliant hues at noon in the garden. And the gentle wash of amber warmth as the sun sinks low on the horizon.

For me, spring is the essence of hope. Of beginning anew and celebrating life in its most intense, yet simplest form.

I imagine that's how God sees us when we are born anew in Him. The dark winter of our souls is replaced with the light of new life in Him. And all of creation rejoices.

Then Jesus said to them,

"A little while longer

the light is with you.

Walk while you have the light,

lest darkness overtake you;

he who walks in darkness

does not know

where he is going."

John 12:35

Thomas Kinkade

For it is
the God

who commanded light

to shine out of darkness,

who has shone in our hearts

to give the light of the knowledge

of the glory of God in the

face of Jesus Christ.

2 Corinthians 4:6

"*For* God so loved
the world

that He gave His only begotten Son,

that whoever believes in Him

should not perish

but have everlasting life....

He who does the truth

comes to the light,

that his deeds may be clearly seen,

that they have been done in God."

John 3:16, 21

And as it is

appointed for men to die once,

but after this the judgment,

so Christ was offered once

to bear the sins of many.

To those who eagerly wait for Him

He will appear a second time,

apart from sin, for salvation.

Hebrews 9:27, 28

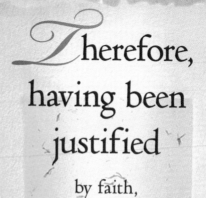

Therefore, having been justified

by faith,

we have peace with God

through our Lord Jesus Christ,

through whom also

we have access by faith

into this grace

in which we stand,

and rejoice in hope

of the glory of God.

Romans 5:1, 2

Thomas
Kinkade

"*Whatever*
I tell you
in the dark,
speak in the light;
and what you hear in the ear,
preach on the housetops."

Matthew 10:27

Jesus said to her,

"I am the resurrection and the life.

He who believes in Me,

though he may die,

he shall live.

And whoever lives

and believes in Me

shall never die.

Do you believe this?"

John 11:25, 26